HOW TO
WRITE A BOOK
AN 11-STEP PROCESS TO BUILD HABITS, STOP PROCRASTINATING, FUEL SELF MOTIVATION, QUIET YOUR INNER CRITIC, BUST THROUGH WRITER'S BLOCK, & LET YOUR CREATIVE JUICES FLOW

— A —

SHORT READ

— BY —

DAVID KADAVY

ALSO BY DAVID KADAVY

Mind Management, Not Time Management: Productivity When Creativity Matters

The Heart to Start: Stop Procrastinating & Start Creating

Design for Hackers: Reverse-Engineering Beauty

© 2018 Kadavy, Inc. All rights reserved.

BONUS MATERIAL

I recently redesigned my life to make writing my top priority. As a result, I quadrupled my writing output. If you'd like to learn what tools I rely on, and get further updates from me, please visit http://kadavy.net/wabtools

TABLE OF CONTENTS

SHEDDING FALSE BELIEFS ABOUT HOW TO WRITE A BOOK 5

STEP 1: START WITH A TINY WRITING HABIT 10

STEP 2: LEARN ABOUT BOOKS BEFORE YOU WRITE A BOOK 11

STEP 4: BUILD AN EMAIL LIST 19

MANTRAS FOR WRITING YOUR BOOK 20

STEP 5: WRITE A BOOK TITLE THAT WILL SELL 23

STEP 6: WRITE AN OUTLINE FOR YOUR BOOK 25

STEP 7: WRITE THE FIRST DRAFT OF YOUR BOOK 26

STEP 8: READ THE FIRST DRAFT OF YOUR BOOK 28

STEP 9: RESTRUCTURE YOUR OUTLINE 30

STEP 10: WRITE YOUR SECOND DRAFT 31

STEP 11: WRITE YOUR FINAL DRAFT 33

CONGRATULATIONS, YOU KNOW HOW TO WRITE A BOOK! 35

SAMPLE CHAPTER: *THE HEART TO START* 37

I NEVER THOUGHT I'd write one book, let alone two. I'm not one of those authors who spent his entire childhood loving to write. I became a writer by accident. If you're wondering how to write a book, the following is what I would suggest.

I'm writing from the perspective of a non-fiction author, but much of what I'll write could be applied to fiction as well. This is not exactly how I did it, but this is how I would do it if I were starting over from scratch. It would have saved me years of struggle in my ten years as an independent creator.

SHEDDING FALSE BELIEFS ABOUT HOW TO WRITE A BOOK

The first step to writing a book is to shed false beliefs about how to write a book. Books can be mysterious. If you haven't written a book, it can be hard to understand what goes into writing a book.

If you don't even personally know an author, books can be even more mysterious. Growing up in a middle-class cul-de-sac in Nebraska, I didn't know authors. I hardly understood that books were created by flesh-and-blood people like myself.

It turns out that writing a book is both harder than I could have imagined, and easier than I could have imagined. It's hard because it takes an amount of dedication that few people put into anything. It's easy because when you get down to it, writing a book is just putting your butt in a chair and laying down words.

FALSE BELIEF #1: WRITING IS ALWAYS HARD.

Writing a book is indeed hard work, and it's not for everyone. This is why you should be honest with yourself about whether you truly want to go through the work of writing a book. There are other ways to author a book, such as Book in a Box.

If you're up for it, know that writing is not always hard. If you don't have much experience writing, chances are it's hard to string together 250 well-written words. When you think about how hard it would be to write 25,000 or 50,000 words, then writing a book seems unbelievably hard.

Getting good at writing isn't a linear process. Writing 25,000 coherent words doesn't have to be one-hundred times as hard as writing 250.

Growing your writing skill is like going to the gym. Sometimes you work out really hard. The hard work you do makes it easier to do the same amount of exercise later on. You'll make more progress by making sure you go to the gym often than you'd make if you overtrained yourself in your first few visits.

You write 250-word pieces a bunch of times, and that gets easy. Then you write a bunch of 500-word pieces, then 1,000. Before you know it, you have the confidence and skill to write a whole book. You can see it in your head as easily as you could see the 250-word piece when you were first starting.

Writing does not always have to be hard, and it gets exponentially easier. The more you write, the easier it gets.

FALSE BELIEF #2: BOOKS ARE WRITTEN STRAIGHT THROUGH.

I used to imagine that to write a book one only needed to sit down and write a book. This is a dangerous false belief that I think many people share.

Why is it dangerous? Because if you think you only need to sit down and write a book, then the only thing that stands between you and a completed book is six months of free time and a secluded cabin in the woods. And who has six months of free time and access to a secluded cabin in the woods? No one.

There are millions of people walking around, fantasizing about the books in their brains, while believing that one day they'll carve out the free time and rent that cabin and write that book. Well, it's not going to happen.

The thing that's dangerous about this belief is it feels good to fantasize about your book, and it feels good to imagine that one day you'll write it. It also feels good to not write, because writing is work and not working feels better than working.

So this belief allows people to not write, and feel good even though they're not writing. Then, one day, they die. And their book is still not written.

You don't just sit down and power through a book. I tried to do this for my first book. I locked myself in my apartment for six months through one of the harshest Chicago winters in history. I was not able to write the book one word after another. Instead, I ended up settling on a compressed version of what I'm about to describe in this book. I got the book done, but I traumatized myself, which is part of the reason it was another six years before I released another book.

Keep in mind, I had even done a decent amount of writing: I had been writing on my blog for six years by the time I got my book deal.

Writing a book is not done straight through, one word after another. It's more about sustained effort, and stitching together a patchwork of knowledge.

FALSE BELIEF #3: DON'T GIVE YOUR WRITING AWAY.

When most people think of writing a book, they imagine writing it, then launching it to a rabid market of readers who want to buy their book.

Because of this fantasy, they believe they shouldn't give their writing away. After all, people are going to pay for their book. They figure if they give away their writing nobody will pay for their writing.

For beginning writers, this causes a creative catch-22 situation: They don't write, because they imagine their writing has to go directly into a book. They can't do that writing, because they haven't written enough to gain the skills to write a book. They end up paralyzed.

Your writing has to compete with every other form of entertainment that exists: This means you're competing against Facebook, *Game of Thrones*, and even sex. These are practically free, so if you insist on only allowing people who have paid to read your writing, you are in for an even more uphill battle than writing a book normally is.

When you're giving away your initial writing for free, you're not really giving it away for "free." Think of it more as a barter exchange: You're exchanging your writing for feedback that will make your writing worth charging for. You're also building a small army of advocates for your writing. Counterintuitively, the people who got your writing for free will also be the first ones to pay for it.

Need examples? E. L. James posted her *Twilight* fan fiction for free before republishing it as *Fifty Shades of Grey*, which sold over 125 million copies, and has been adapted to three feature films. After being rejected by literary agents, Andy Weir put *The Martian* online for free, one chapter at a time. The film adaptation has grossed nearly a quarter of a billion dollars.

Before writing my latest book, I had a call with Nir Eyal, who knows the value of free. He gave away *Hooked: How to Build Habit-Forming Products*, and later got a publishing deal. *Hooked* became a Wall Street Journal best-seller.

In preparation for writing my second book, I was resistant to giving my writing away for free. Nir explained to me that if the ideas are good, they will spread. If they don't, at least you didn't waste years of your life writing something nobody wants to read.

STEP 1: START WITH A TINY WRITING HABIT

Approach writing a book with the image of the Grand Canyon in your mind. You want slow sustained effort over a long period of time. The Grand Canyon was not formed overnight. The Colorado River carved a little bit of it each day.

Something magical happens when you write every day. Writing well may seem impossible at first, but one day it suddenly gets easier. You still have bad days here and there, but you continue to get better.

When I say "every day" I mean at the least every weekday. You can take a couple of days off, but in my experience if you take off more than that you can tell your skill level drops rapidly.

Turn your writing into a habit. Find a ten-minute window each day where you'll have the best chance of completing your habit. Most people keep habits best if they do them in the morning. The chaos of life hasn't gotten a chance to throw all of your intentions off-track. You'll have a better chance of keeping your habit if you put it after a habit you already have. Maybe right after you brush your teeth, you write.

MAKE YOUR WRITING HABIT TINY

Notice that I said you only need a ten-minute window to write. Yes, only ten minutes. This time will eventually grow, like a crack on sidewalk, but you simply need to give writing a little space in your life to start.

Aim for a volume of writing that is way below your ability. I'm a big fan of one-hundred words, but it may be fifty. Keep in mind that you're merely trying to build a habit. It doesn't matter how big the habit is.

When most beginning writers try to build a writing habit, they shoot for something like 1,000 words. They might be able to do it for a day or two, but eventually something gets in the way. The smaller your habit is, the harder it is to make an excuse to not do it.

Yet if you do your habit, chances are you'll gain momentum to do more. Congratulate yourself for doing your habit. Maybe you reward yourself with a sip of coffee.

If you want to keep going after you've hit your target word count, keep going. Do not punish yourself by burning yourself out. Your goal is to feel good about writing today, so you'll want to write again tomorrow. Quit whenever you like.

For more on why "tiny" habits are so powerful, listen to the habits podcast episode I did with Stanford behavioral scientist B.J. Fogg.

STEP 2: LEARN ABOUT BOOKS BEFORE YOU WRITE A BOOK

If you haven't published a book before, you may not know what a book is. I say this because even after I had published one best-seller, I still didn't know what a book was.

It sounds ridiculous to imply that one might not know what a book is. Books are all around us. That is exactly why it's hard to recognize what a book *is*. They're like the air we breathe. We don't think about the complex mixture of molecules that keep us alive with every breath. Similarly, we don't think about how much thought and care goes into making a book worth buying.

A BOOK IS A PRODUCT

A book is a product. A product is something you buy that does something for you. It might be laundry detergent that gets grass stains out. It might be shoes that are comfortable. Then again, it might be shoes that aren't comfortable at all, but that still make you feel good.

A book is no different from any other product. People buy books to get something. They might want to learn something, they might want to make a personal transformation, they might just want to escape for a bit during their train ride to work, or they might buy a book so they can say they're reading it and feel smart at parties.

A book is much more than just a collection of words. The words are arranged in a certain way so that the reader will enjoy it and recommend it to a friend. The words are packaged in a title and a subtitle and a cover so that the reader will want to buy it. The book is categorized and given keywords so that willing readers will be able to find it on Amazon or in the bookstore.

GET YOUR FREE KINDLE-SAMPLE EDUCATION

Once you have a solid writing habit – let's say you've been going steady for about a month of writing consistently – start a new habit. Go to Amazon, and start downloading samples to your Kindle.

If you have some idea of what kind of book you want to write, start with books like that. If you have no idea, look at your favorite book and download Kindle samples of the related books under "customers also bought."

This is the beginning of your free education in the business of books.

Set aside an hour sometime, and read a Kindle sample. Ask yourself, Why would somebody buy this book?

- **Look at the title and subtitle.** How do the title and subtitle tell readers what the book will do for them?
- **Read the first sentence.** Stop for a second and notice your own reaction. How compelled are you to read the next sentence?
- **Read the whole sample.** Try reading it twice: The first time, shut off your brain and let yourself react to the language. The second time, really look at the words and ask yourself why you reacted the way you did (or why you had no reaction at all).

When you reach the end of the sample, ask yourself how compelled you are to keep reading the book (i.e. how compelled you are to buy the book).

Then go look at the Amazon reviews. Look for detailed five-star reviews. Why did someone love it? Look for detailed one-star reviews. Why did someone hate it? Even more valuable, look at the three and four-star reviews. Why did someone *almost* love the book?

Do this on a regular basis. Once in awhile you'll read a sample of a book that you can't help but buy. Take note of that, and pay attention to your internal monologue as you read and decide to buy.

There's no data to be collected here, and there are no spreadsheets to be compiled. Simply make a habit of reading Kindle samples and full books, all while understanding that books are products, and that people buy books for a reason.

I won't go into this in too much detail here. It is an important component of how to write a book, but to get much deeper would be to delve into book marketing. The purpose of this piece is of course to show you how to write a book. If you want to know more about book marketing, listen to my book marketing podcast episode with book-marketing whiz Tucker Max.

STEP 3: BUILD A PUBLISHING HABIT

After you've had a writing habit for a month or so, start building a publishing habit. There are two key points of resistance in writing: Quieting your internal critic enough to actually do the writing, and quieting the imaginary critics you hear when you think about publishing.

Publishing your work is in itself a skill. The more you do it, the better you get at it. You don't necessarily stop getting scared, but you at least learn to look at the fear as a positive sign. If you aren't a little worried before you hit "publish," you probably aren't being open enough in your writing, or you're probably holding something back. (Or you might be a psychopath.)

PUBLISH SOMEWHERE – I RECOMMEND MEDIUM

Publish anywhere people have a chance to see your work. That could be a personal WordPress blog, but I'm personally a big fan of publishing on Medium. Medium gives you two of the most valuable things you could have as a writer: Readers, and feedback.

If you're starting from zero, it will probably be a very long time before anyone is reading your work. When I started writing on Medium, I already had 8,000 followers (from the following I had built over the years on other platforms, such as Twitter). Still, I published a post every day for two months, and it seemed like nobody was reading.

Then, seemingly overnight, I got the hang of it. My first post after two months of daily writing got over 100,000 views, and today I've quadrupled my followers.

Turn your writing habit into a publishing habit. Publish a post of every day on Medium. You can set a lower post-length limit that you allow yourself to exceed, such as 100 words – as in, you can publish 100 words or 1,278 words. Or you can set a target word count that you practice every day – as in, you try to stay around 250 words.

When you set a target word count, such as 250 words, you get better at expressing your ideas in that length. You get better at keeping yourself from going on tangents, and your writing gets tighter. 250, 500, and 1,000-word posts – and multi-thousand-word pieces like this one, all have a different flow to them. It's helpful to master one length before you attempt another length.

USE TAGS TO GET IN FRONT OF READERS

writing

Writing (126K)

Writing Tips (9.1K)

Writing Prompts (4.8K)

Writing Life (2.1K)

Writing Challenge (1.4K)

Medium tags give your work a chance to find readers interested in a topic.

Be sure to add "tags" to your posts so there's a chance someone will read them. As you add a tag while publishing a post, you'll see a little number next to the name of the tag. That tells you how many people are following a tag.

When you're just starting, you want a couple relevant tags that have some audience, but not too much, so there's less competition. Go ahead and throw in a couple relevant tags that have a huge audience, just in case.

READ YOUR COMMENTS

Eventually, people will start commenting on your posts. This is where you start seeing how well your writing is working.

You'll be puzzled how many comments completely miss the point of your article. Even more amazing, there will be comments that are essentially, "Yeah, but did you think about *this*!?" and *this* is directly addressed in your post.

This is where you learn that readers aren't paying close attention. They're riding the bus and reading your post while listening to a podcast and trying not to have inappropriate fantasies about the other people on the bus. Or maybe they're just not that smart.

It doesn't matter. Your job as a writer is to write so engagingly and clearly that your readers turn off their podcasts, sit up in their seats, and pay attention. Then your job is to write so that the thoughts you want to put in their brains successfully make it into their brains.

Yes, some people are at such a low level of intelligence and attention that you have to decide that you just can't reach them. But ultimately it's your responsibility whether your writing connects. If your writing doesn't connect, you won't sell books.

You might freak out the first time someone comments

on your work, especially if they criticize you or try to start a debate. You should think more about understanding the person and what they're saying than you should think about your response. Did they misunderstand something you could have said more clearly? What personal motivations do they have for commenting at all?

You can respond if you want to thoughtful comments, but don't stress about it. For negative comments, take a deep breath, try to understand, look for constructive criticism, and – if there are more productive ways you can use your precious energy – ignore.

REVIEW HIGHLIGHTS

You'll also start seeing highlights on your post. I can't stress enough how valuable these are. This alone gives Medium an edge over any other place you can publish your work.

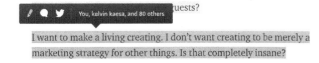

Reviewing your Medium highlights is a great way to see exactly what resonates.

People highlight to make a comment about a passage, to share it on social media, or just to remember or agree with something you've written. You're seeing exactly what connects with people, and exactly what they want to share with others.

Each time you see a highlight someone has made, read it over and over again. Ask yourself what it was about that statement that stood out for them. You'll often find that people highlight stuff that seems obvious or basic to you. You might go through a brilliant, well-thought-out explanation, and it's the conclusion that people highlight.

Over time, you gain a sense of what people will highlight. While you're writing, see if you can tell ahead of time what the most popular highlight will be.

STEP 4: BUILD AN EMAIL LIST

Having an email list – where people can sign up to hear about your work via email – isn't a requirement to write a book. But, it makes going through the work of writing a book worthwhile.

If you have a couple hundred people who you already know are interested in reading your work, it's much easier to find the motivation to write your book.

There are many ways to optimize convincing people to sign up for your email list. Don't let the perfect be the enemy of the good. Start with something simple, like a short message at the end of each post, saying "Want to be the first to know when I publish a new post? [Sign up here »]"

In the future, you can offer some sort of freebie for signing up. I offer tools for optimizing creative output. As you'll see later, I also drove new sign-ups by letting my subscribers read my new book for free, as I wrote it.

Which email marketing platform should you use? For authors, I recommend ConvertKit. I personally use Active Campaign, which is more cumbersome and complicated, but offers a little more control. I have a lot of complicated automations for selling my online courses, so it's worth it for me – though sometimes I have to say I wish I were on Convert-Kit. I wrote a detailed comparison of ConvertKit vs Active Campaign, if you want to learn more.

MANTRAS FOR WRITING YOUR BOOK

I'll take a short break from the "steps" of writing a book to share some useful "mantras" to keep you going. Turning yourself into a writer is a battle with your own mind. You may try to talk yourself out of building a habit, out of making that habit tiny, or out of making a habit out of publishing.

For me, I find it useful to have "mantras:" Things I tell myself every now and then to get out of my own way. Here are some that I find valuable.

BOOK-WRITING MANTRA #1: "THERE'S MORE WHERE THAT CAME FROM."

When you're starting out writing, there's a temptation to treat each line of writing as if it were a drop of liquid gold that must be salvaged. This feeling is made more intense by the fact that you're only shooting to write a small amount of words each day.

Ultimately, you're aiming to be in the mindset that, *There's more where that came from.* Yes, I want to write certain number of words each day, but there's always more. Sometimes I write many thousands of words each day, but I only congratulate myself for the fact that I wrote at all.

BOOK-WRITING MANTRA #2: "I CAN ALWAYS IMPROVE THIS."

One of my proudest accomplishments from becoming a writer is getting comfortable with writing poorly. It can be paralyzing trying to get those first few words onto the page, because your inner critic is laughing so loudly.

By telling yourself, *I can always improve this*, you remind yourself that you will take a second, third, or fourth pass at your writing. You kill perfection paralysis.

BOOK-WRITING MANTRA #3: "IT'S OKAY TO SAY IT AGAIN."

If you feel like you only have one chance to say something, you make it harder to say. You think you've got to get it perfect. You fear your readers will get sick of hearing the same thing again.

Nobody is paying that close of attention, and most people like the reminder anyway. Tell yourself, *It's okay to say it again*. Allow yourself to write about the same subject multiple times. You'll find that you get better and better at writing about that thing.

BOOK-WRITING MANTRA #4: "IT'S BETTER THAN YOU THINK IT IS."

We're the harshest critics of our own work. This is especially true if you're a perfectionist. Your ego wants to nitpick your writing because it keeps you from publishing it.

If you don't publish it, it can't fail. Tell yourself, *It's better than you think it is*. Even if it's not that great, at least you get it out there, and you can improve the next time.

BOOK-WRITING MANTRA #5: "I AM A BRICKLAYER."

Writing is a job. You can spend a lifetime working on your word selection and pacing and storytelling, but ultimately you are laying down words, one after another.

Tell yourself, *I am a bricklayer*. You have a certain amount of bricks you want to lay each day, and after the job is done you can feel like you accomplished something.

BOOK-WRITING MANTRA #6: "THERE'S ALWAYS TOMORROW."

Sometimes you are going to have a hard day. You're going to wake up feeling great, and be shocked to find that you write terribly. Other times, you'll wake up feeling bad, and find that you write well.

It doesn't matter. All that matters is that you wrote. Remind yourself, *There's always tomorrow*. If you keep doing it every day, good days will come.

BOOK-WRITING MANTRA #7: "I WON'T LIVE FOREVER."

This directly contradicts the previous mantra, but it has a different purpose. If you forget that your life is short, you can easily make excuses for not writing.

Remind yourself, *I won't live forever*. If you remember that you can die at any moment, it can give you the extra urgency you need to do your work while you're alive.

STEP 5: WRITE A BOOK TITLE THAT WILL SELL

You may have had a title for your book in mind before you started all of this. If you're anything like me, after studying lots of books, you've realized that's not the right title.

Coming up with a good book title is worth writing a book about. There are so many factors to consider. Here's just a few:

- What keywords will people use to search for the book?
- How does it feel to tell someone you're reading a book of that title?
- Is it an easy title to understand when spoken?
- Does the title sound cool? Does it have a nice rhythm that rolls off the tongue?
- What are secondary meanings of the words in the title? Does it conjure up imagery that supports or detracts from what you want to convey?

Here are some of these phenomena at work:

Play it Away is a book about curing anxiety. Author Charlie Hoehn has said that he didn't want anxiety in the title because it makes people less likely to tell a friend they are reading it.

But, people who are looking for anxiety books (a more

private activity) can find it while searching, because anxiety is in the subtitle: *A Workaholic's Cure for Anxiety*.

(I could go on about whether people want to tell others they're reading a book about "play," or about the badge of honor they might wear while declaring themselves a "workaholic.")

Deep Work passes the "cocktail party test." It feels cool to tell someone that the work you're doing is "deep." It makes you feel important. This is why "deep work" has become its own term people talk about in certain circles.

Deep Work could have easily been called *The Importance of Focus*, and it wouldn't be as sticky.

Loneliness is a good book about an important topic, written by an academic who has dedicated his career to studying that topic. But I bet the title holds back its sales.

Even the author tells an anecdote about being embarrassed about reading an early copy of the book, which said "loneliness" on it, while on a plane.

Again, this is an endlessly-complex topic. I've listed it as a step, but don't let a lack of a good title get in the way of actually writing your book. The right title will become more clear as you write.

To learn more about writing book titles, again I recommend my Tucker Max podcast episode.

STEP 6: WRITE AN OUTLINE FOR YOUR BOOK

When I was in school. Every English teacher confused me. They would ask me to write an outline, *then* write my paper. I always wondered, how can I possibly write an outline if I don't know what I'm going to write? (In my latest book, *The Heart to Start*, I call this "The Linear Work Distortion.")

Here's a couple things I wish somebody would have told me about being a writer: It's much easier to write about what you know. It's also much easier to know something once you've written about it.

By this point, you've been writing every day for a few months, and you've been publishing every day for a couple of those months. Sometimes you've reminded yourself that it's okay to repeat yourself in your writing.

This has constructed a "point of view" in your mind. One post relates to another, and some things overlap. Eventually, you form a point of view about an entire subject. When you have a point of view about a subject, you find that writing an outline about it is much easier.

Write down a bullet-point list of the topics you'd like to cover in your book. Think back to everything you've learned from your Kindle-sample-reading habit. How have the more compelling books started out, and how can you start out in a similar manner?

This isn't something you'll get right the first time. You may try this early on in your writing quest, and find it difficult. If you keep revising your outline every once in awhile, you'll find that it starts to solidify.

Eventually, you'll have an outline that's good enough for a first draft.

STEP 7: WRITE THE FIRST DRAFT OF YOUR BOOK

You've made a habit of writing and publishing, and you've written enough that you have a general outline of what you'd like to say about an entire topic.

Now it's time to write a first draft. You know you're ready to write a first draft because when you look at your outline you can almost see each chapter in your head. You've already written much of what you're about to say. It's like you have a bunch of pieces of fabric and now you're going to stitch them together into a quilt.

Since you can see each chapter in your head and since you've done enough writing that you have a feel for how long each chapter needs to be, you can do a more detailed outline.

Plan out roughly how many words each section will be, and plan out how many words you can write on each day. Put your writing sessions on your calendar. If you've been keeping a writing and publishing habit, it should be easy to know what time works best for you, and to feel confident you can stick to your schedule.

I "lied" to myself in writing the first draft that spawned

The Heart to Start (a technique I call "Motivational Judo," in the book itself). I planned thirty chapters in thirty days (weekdays). I told myself I would write 250–500 words each day. I ended up writing about 1,000 words each day.

250–500 words per chapter would have been fine because I could have expanded upon everything in my second draft. But telling myself that was all I had to write helped me commit to my schedule.

KEEP YOURSELF ACCOUNTABLE

Planning out your writing sessions for your first draft takes a higher level of commitment than your daily writing or publishing habits did.

For one, you're writing more words per day. You're also planning ahead of time what you're going to write. You need to be able to get yourself into the right mindset to write about pre-planned topics, one day after another.

It can be frightening, and writing your first draft will require you to dig in a little more. You can make it easier if you find a way to hold yourself accountable.

Fortunately, you can hold yourself accountable *and* build your audience at the same time. I created a landing page, on which I listed my chapter outline. I promised anyone who signed up to my email list a chapter a day for thirty days (weekdays).

You can create a landing page with a tool such as Lead-

Pages or Thrive Themes (what I used). If you use ConvertKit for your email list, they have built in landing page templates you can use.

Once you have people signed up for your first draft, it's time to stick to your writing schedule. I made sure to stay about a week ahead of schedule. I'd write a really bad draft every morning, I'd let that draft incubate in my brain a little bit, and I'd revisit it in the afternoon of the next day. At the end of each week, I'd schedule the next week's emails in my email autoresponder.

This way of writing a first draft is great, not only because it keeps you accountable, but also because it makes it easy for people to read your book. Most people are busy, and reading a book, especially from an unknown author, is a big commitment. If you can deliver 500 or 1,000 words to their inboxes each day, they can read your book one piece at a time.

STEP 8: READ THE FIRST DRAFT OF YOUR BOOK

It's a wonderful feeling when you finish the first draft of your book. *You have written a book!* Clearly, it has lots of mistakes and room for improvement, but it *is* a book. And now you begin the second draft.

My favorite moments of writing a book are when I print it out. There is something about having a stack of paper full of many thousands of words of your writing that makes the book seem more real than ever. I find it's a great source of motivational fuel.

Print out your first draft. Leave a wide margin on the right side of your document, and print on only one side of each page, so you have space to write. I take it to the Office Depot down the street, and I clamp together the pages with a binder clip. Then, I go sit outside at a cafe in the temperate Medellín air.

Printing out your first draft is an amazing feeling. It also helps you "feel" your book as a reader would.

Reading your book on paper, with no computer and your mobile device hidden away, brings you a new level of focus. You need it, because you're going to take your book in for the first time.

Shut off your brain for a second. Forget about everything you know about the book, and everything you want the book to be. Try to clean the slate, and be a human reacting to your book for the first time.

Try to read through the book one full time without marking much. You aren't worrying about misspelling or grammar. You're just trying to *feel* the book. How does it compare to how it feels to read some of the best Kindle samples you've read?

Now, go through it a second time. Write notes in the margins, or on the back of the pages. You aren't trying to rewrite your prose, you're just thinking about the structure of the book, what you're leaving out, or what seems unnecessary.

Be patient with this phase of evaluating your first draft. You have to let it incubate. The longer you step away from your first draft, the more clearly you'll see what you need to do when you revisit it. In *On Writing*, Stephen King encourages fiction authors to let their first drafts sit in a drawer for six weeks before even looking at them.

You've likely been neglecting some part of your life during writing your first draft, so it's okay to take some time off. Maintain some kind of a writing and reading habit so you don't forget that you are a writer.

I spent a couple of months working on other parts of my business while I let my first draft incubate.

STEP 9: RESTRUCTURE YOUR OUTLINE

When you do return to your book, revisit the outline.

Better yet, sit down with a notebook, and write an outline for the book from scratch, paying no attention to what you remember or don't remember about the book's outline. You'll probably have a crisper and clearer outline than you've ever had before.

You may have to take several cracks at your new outline before it feels right. You may find that you have to restructure your book completely.

If you're writing your first book, it's very common to try to cram too many ideas into your book. Now that you've been studying books regularly, you'll have a better idea of what should stay, and what should get cut.

The Heart to Start came out of my outline for a book tentatively called *Getting Art Done*. Upon reviewing my first draft, I discovered that there was an entire part of my book that was all about getting over starting resistance. I realized that needed to be its own separate book! It didn't fit with the theme of GAD, which was more about optimizing creative output.

STEP 10: WRITE YOUR SECOND DRAFT

By this point, you should have a much better handle on your writing than you did when you started. You needed the tiny habits in the beginning to make it easy to do the activity of writing, which solidified your identity as a writer.

Now that you have a first draft under your belt, it's time

to find a way to get the second draft done. This will probably be much easier. You now have a mound of clay that you can work with.

You need to find a way to keep yourself motivated, and the way to do that may have changed at this point. You may want to announce another daily writing challenge to your email list, or you may feel like you don't need that anymore. You may feel confident that you can simply keep a daily writing habit and get the second draft done.

In the second draft, you're thinking about:

- **Structure.** As the author, you are the tour guide in the jungle of your own mind. The challenge of non-fiction is presenting a complex interconnected network of concepts in a somewhat linear manner. Show your readers you have a plan, that you won't get them lost, and that they won't get eaten by a tiger if they follow you.
- **Opening and value proposition.** Think back to all of those great Kindle samples you've read. Is the opening of your book strong? Does it clearly lay out the concept? Is it clear to the readers how the book will help them? Will it motivate them to buy?
- **Connective tissue.** The outline and flow of concepts are the bone of your book, and then there is the "connective tissue." Are there smooth transitions from the end of one chapter to the beginning of the next? If you pass over a complex subject do you calm readers by letting them know you'll cover it later?
- **Story.** No matter what the subject, your book will be a more enjoyable read if you're paying attention to story. In *The Heart to Start*, I tell my own story of going from cubicle dweller to best-selling author, but each chapter also

has little stories from guests on my podcast, *Love Your Work*. My story is woven throughout the book, while there's a story or two from other creators in each chapter.

I would recommend printing out your book once or twice while working toward a second draft. I personally find it very motivating, and it helps me think about my book on a higher level.

STEP 11: WRITE YOUR FINAL DRAFT

You've written your first draft, you've let it incubate, and you've restructured and rewritten your book. Now it's time to polish it and get it ready to be published.

No matter how perfect you think your book is, you need some kind of editing help. You can hire editors off of sites such as Upwork or Reedsy. How much you spend on an editor is up to you.

Your editor might suggest a restructuring of your book yet again. Or, you might prefer to keep the structure as it is, and focus on spelling, grammar, and punctuation.

You want to strike a balance here: Every book you write is going to be imperfect. How imperfect can you handle it being? Are you willing to invest thousands of dollars and many more months tweaking this book?

If you're a first-time author, even when you call your book "done," there's still so much left for you to learn. You might be better off getting your book done, knowing that your next book will be even better. Remember the mantra,

There's more where that came from.

Also, with Kindle and print-on-demand services like Createspace, you can always update your book later. Pat Flynn released his first book, *Let Go*, then a few years later launched an updated and expanded edition. You can update your Kindle edition a couple times a day if you want (only new customers will get your new edition).

I didn't hire an editor at all for *The Heart to Start*. Instead, I "crowd-edited" it (an idea I got from Nir Eyal). I put my second draft in a Google Doc, and shared it with my email list. My readers got to read the book for free, but it was also easy for them to comment and make corrections.

Some comments were about whether something belonged in the book. Some were grammar and punctuation lessons. Others pointed out typos.

Some of my readers were bona-fide editors. I was very lucky to have a lot of smart readers who were willing to provide comments while reading the book for free. Thanks to the editors, my book turned out really great. I think I've received only one errata note from a reader after publishing *The Heart to Start*, which I quickly fixed.

I was sure to collect the names of everyone who provided useful comments. I put them in the acknowledgements section of the book, because, after all, they were my editors! A nice bonus effect from this was that they were then even more invested in the success of the book. If you're in the acknowledgements of a book, naturally you want it to succeed.

CONGRATULATIONS, YOU KNOW HOW TO WRITE A BOOK!

When you think you've picked up all of the changes, print out your book one last time. It's really a thrill to have a stack of words that you've written. You can publish it anywhere: Kindle, iBooks, Google Play, Createspace – or you can sell it directly to your readers!

Congratulations, you've written a book! The most powerful thing I've felt after writing a book is the confidence that I can do it again. Like riding a bike or salsa dancing, you now have a new skill that you can use over and over again for the rest of your life.

Now that you know how to write a book, what are you waiting for? Go ahead and write it! (If that's easier said than done, I have a book for that: It's called *The Heart to Start*, and it will help you overcome fear, self-doubt, and perfectionism to finally make your work real.)

CLICK ON A STAR RATING?

Now that you're done, do you have a second to click on a star rating on Amazon?

Obviously you don't have to do it, but it helps me write more books, and it helps others decide if this book is right for them.

All it takes is a click at http://kadavy.net/wabstar. If you have moment to write a word or two, that's great. But even just a click helps.

Thanks so much for reading.

David

SAMPLE CHAPTER

THE *HEART* TO *START*

DAVID KADAVY

STOP

PROCRASTINATING

& START

CREATING

PROLOGUE

The first step to controlling your world is to control your culture…. To write the books. Make the music. Shoot the films. Paint the art.

—Chuck Palahniuk

I'll start off by introducing the elephant in the room: You don't need this book to get started. If you can put this book down and start creating your art, then that's exactly what you should do. Write your first novel, record your first album, or build your first company. If you're capable of starting now, I hope you're flipping through the first few pages of this book, and haven't spent your hard-earned cash. It was nice talking to you, and I'd love to see what you make.

For me, it's never been that simple. I've been an independent creator for ten years now, making a living from writing, podcasting, and teaching what I learn along the way. I still remember the first time I met a real "starter." He was an older neighborhood kid who was running a snow removal business. As he sipped on a Coca Cola at my high school graduation party, I couldn't stop drilling him with questions. *How did you rebuild the engine on that truck? How did you install the snow plow? How did you find your customers?* He kept shrugging his shoulders and giving me the same frustrating answer: "I just *did* it."

As I started working for myself more than a decade ago, I was hearing this story, in the form of advice, over and over again. It seemed to be all anyone in Silicon Valley could tell me. There was no end to the number of books I could read, speeches I could watch, or podcasts I could listen to that all told me the same thing: *Just get started*. It's good advice if you can follow it, but I was always left wondering: "Yeah, but *how* do I start?"

IN THE FALL of 2016 I settled into my sound studio and logged onto Skype. As I waited for the call to connect, I took a deep breath to calm my racing heart. I was about to interview one of my heroes for my podcast, *Love Your Work*. Like the neighbor kid, James Altucher is a real starter. He's started more than twenty companies. He's written eighteen books, including the *Wall Street Journal* bestseller *Choose Yourself*. He hosts a top-ranked podcast, on which he has interviewed Coolio, Sir Richard Branson, and Sara Blakely.

I go into each interview hoping to get a superpower from my guest. I wanted to find out how James became so prolific. He seemed like the best person I could ask about starting.

Yet as I talked to James, I grew frustrated. It seemed as if he never struggled with starting. He talked about starting one of his many businesses. He said he simply wrote a short business plan and emailed it to people. I asked him about finding the courage to share his embarrassing stories online – did he ever worry about what other people would think? He said he didn't. I asked him about whittling his possessions down to fifteen things, throwing away even his college diploma. Did he ever wonder if he was going crazy? "No, never."

I wasn't finding what I was looking for, so I lost my patience. "This is something I want to figure out about you, James," I interrupted. "I think what holds a lot of people back a lot of times is they don't think big. And if they do start thinking big, they start to question themselves. So I'm wondering: Is this an inherent thing to you, or was there any particular period of time where you didn't think that way and you started to?"

James paused for a moment. "I always thought I could do anything," he said. "I was in second grade, writing books that I thought were going to get published and be bestsellers. I always thought that nothing stood in my way."

It didn't look like I would be getting James's superpower. If he always thought he could do anything, what could he teach someone like me? I still had another forty-five minutes with him, so I resolved to dig deeper. "I feel like…a lot of people," I said, "have these little glimpses of ideas or dreams or fantasies in their heads and then it just goes right over them. They don't realize that the thing that they just fantasized about is something that they could actually go ahead and do."

Then James pointed out something that should have

been obvious. "You follow a lot of ideas. You said you're from Omaha, Nebraska. But now you're sitting in Colombia…doing a podcast with me and I'm six-thousand miles from you…. You're doing this amazing science-fiction thing right now…. So let me ask you a question: Did you just suddenly quit your job and move from Omaha to Colombia? Like, what happened?"

James had a point. Here I was grilling him about starting, but I had clearly made many starts myself. I had started companies, written a bestselling book, and started my podcast. Several weeks prior to our conversation, like James, I had also sold all of my possessions. I moved to South America.

UNLIKE JAMES, I did not always believe I could do anything. In fact, it was as if "anything" didn't exist. Growing up, each book I read, each movie I watched, and each Nintendo game I played may as well have been one of the crab apples growing on the tree in the backyard. It was part of the natural environment. It grew from another species. It never dawned on me that these things were made by mortal humans like me. I never imagined that my work could be less like the bleary-eyed, early-morning processions to school and more like the summers I passed drawing or reading in my room. As far as I could tell, it never dawned on anyone in the quiet cul-de-sac where I grew up – except maybe for the kid with the snow plow.

By the time I did realize it was an option to make my

art – whether it was a painting, a website, or a snow removal business – I had decades of mental programming to undo. I had never considered doing anything other than what I was told. It was assumed that I would do my homework and not talk in class and fill out the proper standardized-test bubbles with a No. 2 pencil. Just what all of this would get me was unclear. It wasn't until I found myself sitting in a beige cubicle that I ever thought to ask.

When I did finally start following my own ideas, this mental programming served as walls of a labyrinth of fears and mental distortions. I feared the judgment of others. I doubted my abilities. I struggled with motivation. I escaped into distractions.

I'm sure James has faced these same obstacles to starting, but somehow he has made overcoming them look easy. It reminds me of the motivation for writing my first book, *Design for Hackers*. A friend told me that every time he asked a designer how to make a beautiful website or logo design, he always got a shoulder shrug, and an unsatisfying response: "I guess you have it, or you don't."

If there's something that comes naturally to me, it's being skeptical of "you have it, or you don't." New research in psychology has shown that I'm right. People who believe they can learn, actually can ("growth mindset"). People who don't believe they can learn, struggle to learn ("fixed mindset"). We used to believe that the brain stopped changing at a certain age, but now we know it never stops changing.

I've seen firsthand that people can do things they don't seem naturally inclined to do. Since writing my first book, I've gotten emails from many self-proclaimed "programmer-types," thrilled that they can finally make beautiful designs. One of these emails was even from a color-blind software developer. He had physical limitations to distinguishing colors, but he simply needed to be shown a new way of understanding color. He now makes money on the side from website themes he designed.

IN THIS BOOK, I will deconstruct starting for those who struggle with the advice, *just get started*. Whether you dream of writing a novel, starting a company, or jumping a motorcycle across the Grand Canyon, I'll show you how to find the heart to start.

The first section of the book will introduce you to the laws of art. You feel a force that compels you to make your art, but what forces keep it inside you?

The second section will help you find the fuel. Where can you search for ideas with enough power to keep you moving, even when things get tough?

The third and final section will help you win by beginning. How do you hold yourself back from starting, and how can you overcome those mental barriers to make a start that will propel you through the finish line?

The main thread of this book is my own story. Through a series of short vignettes, I'll take you through how I've overcome my own fears, doubts, perfectionism, and distractions to start over and over again. I'll take you from Nebraska, to Silicon Valley, to Chicago and Costa Rica, and to where I sit right now, in Colombia. I'll take you through my journey as a cubicle-dweller, to a blogger, to a designer-turned-bestselling-author. Though I've made many starts over the years, the story revolves around what I still believe to be my simplest yet most important start.

Each chapter shows you how other creators and entrepreneurs have used the same phenomena to start. From Evel Knievel to Maya Angelou, from Ed Sheeran to J. K. Rowling, they've all started many times, and they've all overcome the same barriers you and I face. You'll also hear from the podcast guests I've interviewed in more than one hundred episodes of *Love Your Work*, from Seth Godin, from behavioral scientist Dan Ariely, from a Hollywood screenwriter, from a chef, from a creator of a hit board game, and from many others.

With each beginning, there is an end in mind. If you're going to find the heart to start, you need some sense of what it is you're going to start. It might as well be some special thing that nobody else can offer. That's what we'll find in the next chapter.

Buy *The Heart to Start* on Amazon at
http://kadavy.net/wabhts

ABOUT THE AUTHOR

David Kadavy (@kadavy) is a bestselling author, blogger, podcaster, and speaker. Through his blogging at *kadavy.net* and his podcast, *Love Your Work*, he helps people find satisfaction through following their crafts, even if it takes them down unconventional paths. David's writing has appeared in *Quartz*, *Observer*, *Inc.com*, *The Huffington Post*, *McSweeny's Internet Tendency*, and *Upworthy*. He has spoken in eight countries, including appearances at SXSW and TEDx. He lives in Medellín, Colombia.

Made in the USA
Las Vegas, NV
16 February 2022